NEW EVERY DAY

30 DEVOTIONS FOR OLDER PEOPLE BY RITA MCLAUGHLAN

God's Great Faithfulness

Other *New Every Day* titles
God's Unfailing Love

I will sustain you

'*Listen to me, O house of Jacob, all you who remain of the house of Israel, you whom I have upheld since you were conceived, and have carried since your birth. Even to your old age and grey hairs I am he, I am he who will sustain you. I have made you and I will carry you; I will sustain you and I will rescue you. To whom will you compare me or count me equal? To whom will you liken me that we may be compared?' Isaiah 46:3–5*

God is speaking here to His people, Israel, comforting them in a time when there was imminent danger and uncertainty in their land. God doesn't change. His words are just as true now and apply to all His people who love and serve Him today.

God has been with you all your life, even during those times when perhaps you forgot Him, when you were disobedient or careless and didn't serve Him as you should. Look again at the words in the scripture above. What is He promising you? Our God is incomparable. He has no equal, is always loving and is always true to His word.

Prayer:
Thank You, God, for Your promises. I trust You, Lord, to take care of me and sustain me every day. Amen.

His compassions never fail

*B*ecause of the LORD's great love we are not consumed, for his compassions never fail. They are new every morning; great is your faithfulness. I say to myself, 'The LORD is my portion; therefore I will wait for him.'

For men are not cast off by the Lord forever. Though he brings grief, he will show compassion, so great is his unfailing love. For he does not willingly bring affliction or grief to the children of men. *Lamentations 3:22–24,31–33*

What is the first thing you think of when you wake up in the morning? A cup of tea, the weather, a list of things you have to do that day, how you are feeling …? God tells us that His compassions are *new* every morning. So, however you feel, whatever you will face today, His loving compassion reaches out to you, whatever your circumstances.

God is always faithful. His love for you never fails. It is there for you at the beginning of each day and throughout each day. That is a promise worth thinking about when you wake each morning.

Prayer:
Thank You, Father God, that Your loving compassion for me is new this morning and every morning. Please help me to remember that, and to thank You each day. Amen.

Renewal of strength

*T*he LORD is the everlasting God, the Creator of the ends of the earth. He does not faint or grow weary; his understanding is unsearchable. He gives power to the faint, and strengthens the powerless. Even youths will faint and be weary, and the young will fall exhausted; but those who wait for the LORD shall renew their strength, they shall mount up with wings like eagles, they shall run and not be weary, they shall walk and not faint. *Isaiah 40:28b–31 (NRSV)*

God never gets tired. Our friends and family may sometimes be too tired or too busy to offer a helping hand, but God is never too tired to listen to us or to help us. He never grows weary of our prayers but loves to hear and to answer when we call upon Him. Even young, strong people get exhausted at times and as we grow older, simple tasks or journeys can seem to sap our strength more quickly than before. But the promise is the same for us as it is for the young: '… those who hope in the LORD will renew their strength.'

Prayer:
Thank You, Lord, that You hear me always. Please renew my strength today so that I may do whatever You want me to do for You. Amen.

God does not forget

*G*od is not unjust; he will not forget your work and the love you have shown him as you have helped his people and continue to help them. We want each of you to show this same diligence to the very end, in order to make your hope sure. We do not want you to become lazy, but to imitate those who through faith and patience inherit what has been promised. *Hebrews 6:10–12*

All the love you have shown to God and to His people throughout your life is stored up in His memory. He is just – He will not forget your work. That is a firm promise, but it doesn't mean that you can rest on your laurels and become lazy now! The older generation can still show their love to God by being loving and compassionate to the young ones. In our manner, in our speech, in our actions and perhaps most of all in our prayers, we can be diligent in serving God still. He has work for us to do today.

To think about:
'If we confess our sins, he is faithful and just and will forgive us our sins and purify us from all unrighteousness.' (1 John 1:9)
God is indeed just – He forgives all the sin we have said sorry for and sees and remembers our love for Him and for His people.

God always with us

*Y*et I am always with you; you hold me by my right hand. You guide me with your counsel, and afterwards you will take me into glory. Whom have I in heaven but you? And earth has nothing I desire besides you. My flesh and my heart may fail, but God is the strength of my heart and my portion forever. *Psalm 73:23–26*

At the beginning of this psalm, Asaph, one of King David's music directors, confesses his envy of the prosperity of the wicked. Now, near the end of the psalm, he realises that this earth has nothing he desires more than God Himself. He counts his blessings: in this life God is always with him, holding him by the hand and guiding him. But above all, at the end of his life, God will take him into glory to be with Him forever.

These promises are true for you, too. God is with you now and you will be with Him forever. That is something to look forward to! God is your strength.

Prayer:
Thank You, Father, that I have such a glorious hope, both for now and for the future. Thank You that I will be with You forever. Amen.

A place prepared

'*D*o not let your hearts be troubled. Believe in God, believe also in me. In my Father's house there are many dwelling-places. If it were not so, would I have told you that I go to prepare a place for you? And if I go and prepare a place for you, I will come again and will take you to myself, so that where I am, there you may be also. And you know the way to the place where I am going.' *John 14:1–4 (NRSV)*

The disciples were puzzled and distressed because Jesus had told them He would be leaving them. He comforted them by telling them that He was going to prepare a place for them and that He would take them to be with Him. They didn't understand then but we can understand now because we know that Jesus died on the cross for our sins. He rose again and went up to heaven. That is where He is now, and that is where we will be – with Him forever in the place prepared for us. That is His promise to those who believe in Him.

Prayer:
Lord Jesus, I trust in You. Thank You for Your promise that You have prepared a place for me in heaven. Amen.

God's name – I AM

*G*od said to Moses, 'I AM WHO I AM. This is what you are to say to the Israelites: "I AM has sent me to you."' God also said to Moses, 'Say to the Israelites, "The Lord, the God of your fathers – the God of Abraham, the God of Isaac and the God of Jacob – has sent me to you." This is my name forever, the name by which I am to be remembered from generation to generation.' *Exodus 3:14–15*

God is ever present. He is always the same, never changing. That is why, when Moses asked Him His name, He gave it as, 'I AM'; not 'I was' or 'I will be', but 'I AM', yesterday, today, forever. There are many names for God in the Bible – the Almighty, Jehovah, Lord, Saviour, Father, and lots more. But perhaps 'I AM' is the strongest, the one which most describes Him as God who has always been, and God who always will be, who has everything in His hands until the end of time and beyond. This is the God we worship. This is the God who loves you and takes care of you every day.

To think about:
Reflect on God's name, 'I AM'. For the next seven days we will find out how Jesus used the name, 'I AM'.

'I am the bread of life'

*T*hen Jesus said to them, 'Very truly, I tell you, it was not Moses who gave you the bread from heaven, but it is my Father who gives you the true bread from heaven. For the bread of God is that which comes down from heaven and gives life to the world.' They said to him, 'Sir, give us this bread always.' Jesus said to them, 'I am the bread of life. Whoever comes to me will never be hungry, and whoever believes in me will never be thirsty.' *John 6:32–35 (NRSV)*

Jesus was talking to the crowd who, the day before, had seen him feed over five thousand people with bread and fish. They were amazed at the miracle, but Jesus wanted them to understand that spiritual food is even more important than food that feeds our bodies. He often spoke in picture language and here he uses the example of bread, one of the familiar, staple foods of the people's diet. Bread was essential to their physical existence. Jesus declared Himself to be essential to their spiritual lives.

Those who believe in Jesus will draw strength from Him every day and will know His invigorating, abundant life within them.

Prayer:
Lord Jesus, please help me to feed on You day by day and to receive renewal of inner strength. Amen.

'I am the light of the world'

*W*hen Jesus spoke again to the people, he said, 'I am the light of the world. Whoever follows me will never walk in darkness, but will have the light of life.' *John 8:12*

The LORD is my light and my salvation – whom shall I fear? The LORD is the stronghold of my life – of whom shall I be afraid? *Psalm 27:1*

Think about different sources of light: the light from the sun gives life to this world; light from a torch shows the way along a dark street and keeps you from stumbling; the light in your house enables you to live life normally even though it is dark outside; light from a fire gives warmth in the house or burns up the rubbish in the garden. Light is stronger than darkness – as soon as a light is switched on, the darkness disappears and you can see clearly. Light drives away fear. In the dark there may be all sorts of real or imagined dangers, but light enables you to face up to whatever life holds for you.

What a wonderful picture Jesus gives us! He is our light – we can see clearly and need never be afraid when we follow Him.

Prayer:
Jesus, You are the Light of the world, and I thank You that You are my Light. Amen.

'I am the gate'

'*I* tell you the truth, the man who does not enter the sheep pen by the gate, but climbs in by some other way, is a thief and a robber.'

Therefore Jesus said again, 'I tell you the truth, I am the gate for the sheep. All who ever came before me were thieves and robbers, but the sheep did not listen to them. I am the gate; whoever enters through me will be saved. He will come in and go out, and find pasture.'
John 10:1,7–9

You may have seen shepherds with their sheep dogs rounding up their flocks and guiding them into the pen through the one entrance. An Eastern shepherd in Jesus' time would often then lie down across the entrance to the sheep pen to keep thieves and wild animals out and the sheep safe. In word pictures, Jesus was telling His followers that there is only one way into the kingdom of God, through Himself. It was Jesus, the Son of God, who gave His life on the cross so that we might enter the kingdom. Those who believe in Him will be safe. There is no other gate into the kingdom of God.

Prayer:
Thank You, Jesus, for giving Your life for me and for being the Gateway into the kingdom of God. Amen.

'I am the good shepherd'

'*I* am the good shepherd; I know my sheep and my sheep know me – just as the Father knows me and I know the Father – and I lay down my life for the sheep.' *John 10:14–15*

In the Middle East the shepherd goes ahead of his flock and the sheep follow him. Where there are several flocks together, the sheep all know which shepherd to follow and the shepherds know their own sheep individually. It is very comforting to know that Jesus, the Good Shepherd, knows you by name – He knows all about you. He knows when you are happy and when you are sad, when you are well and when you are hurting, when life is easy and when life is difficult. He cares about you and for you in all circumstances.

Just as the shepherd spends his life with his sheep, so Jesus is with you all the time. It is a very close relationship, giving you the security you need. He laid down His life for you so that you may receive forgiveness and belong in the safety of His flock.

To think about:
'The Lord is my shepherd, I shall not be in want.'
(Psalm 23:1)
If you are able, turn in your Bible to Psalm 23 and read the whole psalm today.

'I am the way and the truth and the life'

*T*homas said to [Jesus], 'Lord we don't know where you are going, so how can we know the way?' Jesus answered, 'I am the way and the truth and the life. No-one comes to the Father except through me. If you really knew me, you would know my Father as well. From now on, you do know him and have seen him.'
John 14:5–6

There is only one way to God, the Father, and that is through Jesus Christ, His Son. Jesus gave His life on the cross so that we might be cleansed from sin and enter into a relationship with our holy God. Jesus is the Way.

There is only one truth. There are many gods in many different religions in the world but only one true God. Jesus is the living reality, the fulfilment of all the promises in the Bible. Jesus is the Truth.

Jesus came to give us life, not just for this world, but eternal life, so that we can be with Him forever. Jesus is the Life.

Prayer:
Thank You, Jesus, that You not only came to show us the way to God, but that You are the Way Yourself. Thank You that You are the Truth, and thank You for giving me life. Amen.

'I am the true vine'

'*I* am the vine, you are the branches. Those who abide in me and I in them bear much fruit, because apart from me you can do nothing. Whoever does not abide in me is thrown away like a branch and withers; such branches are gathered, thrown into the fire, and burned. If you abide in me, and my words abide in you, ask for whatever you wish, and it will be done for you. My Father is glorified by this, that you bear much fruit and become my disciples.' *John 15:5–8 (NRSV)*

There were many vineyards in Israel and people would have been familiar with the cultivation and pruning of vines. A strong branch draws its nourishment from the stem and bears fruit. A branch that is broken off is good for nothing but to be burnt.

Jesus likens a Christian to that strong branch, firmly linked to Him, drawing life from Him and bearing fruit for Him. As we draw nourishment from Him day by day, through reading His Word, listening to His voice and talking to Him, so the fruits of love, joy and answered prayer will be seen in our lives.

Prayer:
Please keep me firmly fixed in You, Lord, day by day, so that fruit may be seen in my life. Amen.

'I am the resurrection and the life'

*J*esus said to [Martha], 'I am the resurrection and the life. He who believes in me will live, even though he dies; and whoever lives and believes in me will never die. Do you believe this?' 'Yes, Lord,' she told him, 'I believe that you are the Christ, the Son of God, who was to come into the world.' *John 11:25–27*

Martha's brother, Lazarus, had died and his two sisters were naturally very upset. They both believed that if Jesus had been there He would have healed Lazarus. Jesus, however, had something even more important to show Martha and Mary: not only could He heal the sick, He could also raise the dead. Lazarus received his life again.

More importantly than that, Jesus declared Himself to *be* the resurrection and the life. He Himself came back to life three days after He died on the cross, and He is alive now, in heaven. Because of this, we who believe in Him will also have eternal life. Our bodies may deteriorate and die but we ourselves will go on living – with Him forever.

Prayer:
Dear Lord Jesus, please help me to understand and believe this wonderful truth, that all who trust in You will live with You in eternity. Amen.

Noah, the obedient

*N*oah was a righteous man, blameless among the people of his time, and he walked with God. God saw how corrupt the earth had become ... So God said to Noah, 'I am going to put an end to all people, for the earth is filled with violence because of them. I am surely going to destroy both them and the earth. So make yourself an ark of cypress wood; make rooms in it and coat it with pitch inside and out.'

Noah did everything just as God commanded him.
Genesis 6:9,12–14,22

Building the ark was no small task for Noah and his sons. It was the length of one and a half football pitches and the height of a four-storey block of flats – the size of an ocean-going liner! Noah must have wondered, during the building, what kind of catastrophe God was going to bring about on the earth and how the ark would save them. But he persevered and finished the task he had been set.

We know the end of the story. A tremendous flood on the earth destroyed all living creatures except those in the ark with Noah.

Noah's obedience saved his family.

Prayer:
Dear Lord, please help me to be obedient to Your commands, however small or however big they may be. Amen.

Abraham the faithful

*T*he LORD had said to Abram, 'Leave your country, your people and your father's household and go to the land I will show you.'

So Abram left, as the LORD had told him; and Lot went with him. Abram was seventy-five years old when he set out from Haran. *Genesis 12:1,4*

By faith Abraham, when called to go to a place he would later receive as his inheritance, obeyed and went, even though he did not know where he was going. By faith he made his home in the promised land like a stranger in a foreign country ... *Hebrews 11:8–9*

Abraham's faith in God makes him stand out among the great men we read about in the Bible. He was another, like Noah, who obeyed when God gave him instructions. He had the faith to leave his home and his family and set out on a journey, not knowing where he would end up, and thus he established a foothold for the Jewish people in the promised land of Canaan.

Abraham did not see the fulfilment of God's promise but his life of faith paved the way for future generations. His faith produced a lasting effect for the Jewish people and is an example for us to follow.

Prayer:
Lord, teach me to trust You, and to move in faith as Abraham did. Amen.

Gideon the brave

*G*ideon was beating out wheat in a winepress, to hide it from the Midianites. The angel of the LORD appeared to him and said to him, 'The LORD is with you, you mighty warrior.' Gideon answered him, 'But sir, if the LORD is with us, why then has all this happened to us? And where are all his wonderful deeds that our ancestors recounted to us … But now the LORD has cast us off, and given us into the hand of Midian.' Then the LORD turned to him and said, 'Go in this might of yours and deliver Israel from the hand of Midian; I hereby commission you.'
Judges 6:11b–14 (NRSV)

Wheat would normally have been threshed in the open air so that the wind could carry away the chaff. But Gideon was afraid. He was hiding in a winepress. His question to the Lord is understandable – 'If You are with us, Lord, why are we suffering constant raids from the Midianites who ruin our crops and kill our livestock?' His fear is understandable, too, yet God called him a 'mighty warrior' and told him to go and fight to save His people.

God does not often call the strong and brave to fulfil His purposes. Gideon was weak and afraid but brave enough to trust God and go because God sent him.

Thought:
Trust God and go in the strength you have.

Joseph the forgiving

*W*hen [Joseph's] brothers saw that their father loved him more than any of them, they hated him and could not speak a kind word to him.

His brothers then came and threw themselves down before him. 'We are your slaves,' they said. But Joseph said to them, 'Don't be afraid. Am I in the place of God? You intended to harm me, but God intended it for good to accomplish what is now being done, the saving of many lives. So then, don't be afraid. I will provide for you and your children.' And he reassured them and spoke kindly to them. *Genesis 37:4; 50:18–21*

Joseph's brothers hated him and tried first of all to kill him, then sold him to traders who took him into Egypt. There he rose to a high position and was able to save many thousands of people from famine.

Years later his brothers came to him for food and instead of being cruel to them as they had been to him, Joseph was kind and provided them with food for their families. Joseph was in a position to pay his brothers back for the way they had treated him when he was young but he chose not to. He chose to forgive. He chose to be kind.

Prayer:
Father, please help me to forgive. Amen.

Job the unshakeable

'*I* know that my Redeemer lives, and that in the end he will stand upon the earth. And after my skin has been destroyed, yet in my flesh I will see God; I myself will see him with my own eyes – I, and not another. How my heart yearns within me!' *Job 19:25–27*

Job was in terrible trouble – he had lost his family and all his livestock in various disasters. Then he was struck down by a seemingly incurable disease and was in a lot of pain and discomfort. His wife told him to, 'Curse God and die' (Job 2:9).

'[Job] replied, "You are talking like a foolish woman. Shall we accept good from God, and not trouble?"' (Job 2:10). Job's friends came and sat with him, trying to help with long speeches, but only succeeded in making the situation worse. In all of this, however, Job never lost his faith in God. Whether he lived or died he knew three things for certain:

- that God, the Redeemer, lives;
- that one day God would come and stand on the earth;
- that he would one day see God with his own eyes.

Thought:
Job's faith in God was unshakeable. No matter what happens in our lives or in the world, God does not change.

Thomas the believer

*T*hen Jesus said to Thomas, 'Put your finger here; see my hands. Reach out your hand and put it into my side. Stop doubting and believe.' Thomas said to him, 'My Lord and my God!' Then Jesus told him, 'Because you have seen me, you have believed; blessed are those who have not seen and yet have believed.'
John 20:27–29

We usually think of Thomas as 'Doubting Thomas'. He would not believe that Jesus had risen from the dead when the other disciples told him they had seen Him. Thomas wanted proof. He wanted to see and feel for himself the nail marks in Jesus' hands and the wound in His side. He wanted to be sure before he committed himself.

Jesus was kind to Thomas – He showed him the nail marks and told him very firmly to stop doubting. Immediately Thomas changed his attitude and took a giant step forward in faith, declaring, 'My Lord and my God!'

Thomas believed because he had seen with his own eyes, but Jesus went on to say that those, like you and me, who have not seen Jesus yet still believe, are especially blessed.

To think about:
'But these [things] are written that you may believe that Jesus is the Christ, the Son of God, and that by believing you may have life in his name.' (John 20:31)

Barnabas the encourager

*J*oseph ... whom the apostles called Barnabas (which means Son of Encouragement), sold a field he owned and brought the money and put it at the apostles' feet.

When [Paul] came to Jerusalem, he tried to join the disciples, but they were all afraid of him ... But Barnabas took him and brought him to the apostles.

... the church at Jerusalem ... sent Barnabas to Antioch. When he arrived and saw the evidence of the grace of God, he was glad and encouraged them all to remain true to the Lord with all their hearts.
Acts 4:36–37; 9:26–27; 11:22–23

Barnabas' real name was Joseph, but the nickname the apostles gave him stuck. He is referred to as 'Barnabas' (Son of Encouragement) in the book of Acts whenever he is mentioned, and he certainly lived up to his name. In our readings today we can see how he encouraged the church and individuals by his lifestyle, his actions and his words.

Later in the book we read that, when Paul dismissed a young man called Mark, Barnabas took Mark under his wing and helped him along. An encouraging word and a helping hand make all the difference to someone who is struggling.

Prayer:
Please help me, Father, to be an encourager, just as Barnabas was. Amen.

The prayer of an old king

My rock of refuge

*I*n you, O LORD, I have taken refuge; let me never be put to shame. Rescue me and deliver me in your righteousness; turn your ear to me and save me. Be my rock of refuge, to which I can always go; give the command to save me, for you are my rock and my fortress. Deliver me, O my God, from the hand of the wicked, from the grasp of evil and cruel men. *Psalm 71:1–4*

Psalm 71 is the prayer of an elderly man, probably King David in his declining years. The psalmist remembers that he has always taken refuge in the Lord. God has been his rock and his fortress, his protection throughout his life, but now, as his strength begins to fail, he cries out again for help. Possibly there were enemies taking advantage of the king's decline and he felt the need for extra deliverance.

As we grow older we do meet with new challenges, new difficulties in life, and God is always ready to help us. He understands our changing circumstances and we can run to Him, our rock and our fortress, for protection and comfort at all times.

Prayer:
Dear God, thank You that You have always been my Rock of Refuge. Please help me now, at this time of my life, to trust You still. Amen.

My confidence

*F*or you have been my hope, O Sovereign LORD, my confidence since my youth. From my birth I have relied on you; you brought me forth from my mother's womb. I will ever praise you. I have become like a portent to many, but you are my strong refuge. My mouth is filled with your praise, declaring your splendour all day long. *Psalm 71:5–8*

As he looks back over the past the psalmist is filled with praise. He is certain that God has been with him throughout his life, even before birth. God was his hope and his confidence in his youth. If this psalm was indeed written by King David, we remember that when he was a teenager he killed the giant, Goliath, with his slingshot, and gave the glory to God even then.

Whoever wrote this psalm, however, was a man whose whole life had been filled with praise to God and complete confidence in Him. In his old age, he is still declaring his admiration for the One who has been his support and his refuge all through the years. We can do the same.

To think about:
What can you praise God for in your past? How can you praise Him today? We can surely praise God all day long.

My help

*D*o not cast me away when I am old; do not forsake me when my strength is gone. For my enemies speak against me; those who wait to kill me conspire together. They say, 'God has forsaken him; pursue him and seize him, for no one will rescue him.' Be not far from me, O God; come quickly, O my God, to help me. May my accusers perish in shame; may those who want to harm me be covered with scorn and disgrace. *Psalm 71:9–13*

Once again the psalmist cries out to God for help. His enemies are conspiring against him and he does not feel strong enough in his old age to do battle against them as he would have done when he was young. But he still trusts in God. He tells God what is happening and how he feels.

God is always ready to listen to us and although He already knows all about us, He wants us to talk to Him as children would talk to their father. So, tell your heavenly Father about all your needs and concerns and ask Him to help you.

Thought:
The psalmist wished harm on his accusers, but Jesus gave us a new command: 'Love your enemies and pray for those who persecute you ...' (Matthew 5:44)

My hope

*B*ut as for me, I shall always have hope; I will praise you more and more. My mouth will tell of your righteousness, of your salvation all day long, though I know not its measure. I will come and proclaim your mighty acts, O Sovereign Lord; I will proclaim your righteousness, yours alone. *Psalm 71:14–16*

Yesterday we read about certain troubles and dangers that the psalmist was facing, and how he cried out to the Lord for help. Today we see that he still had hope and was filled with praise. He was not afraid to speak out his praises of the Lord who had been his hope and his help throughout his life.

There are three 'I will's in this section: 'I will praise', 'I will come', 'I will proclaim', and also, 'My mouth will tell …'. The psalmist is quite definite in his determination to proclaim the righteousness, salvation and mighty acts of his Lord. What an example we have in this old man! He didn't waste time grumbling and complaining about his situation. He first asked God for help, then praised and spoke out to all around about his hope in his mighty Sovereign Lord.

Prayer:
I praise You, Lord. You are my hope and, with Your help, I will praise and proclaim Your might all my life. Amen.

My teacher

*S*ince my youth, O God, you have taught me, and to this day I declare your marvellous deeds. Even when I am old and grey, do not forsake me, O God, till I declare your power to the next generation, your might to all who are to come. *Psalm 71:17–18*

Once again the psalmist remembers his younger days, how the Lord taught him then and throughout his life. Over the years we are continually learning new things about God, about ourselves, about how to live our lives and how to deal with different situations. In our old age there are still new things to learn.

But the psalmist wants to be able to pass on his knowledge of God's power to the younger generation. We need gentleness and wisdom to do this. Young people need to know about God's love, His power, His forgiveness, His saving grace, and we who have experienced His presence can tell them. Think about the younger generation in your own family and ask God for opportunities to talk to them about Jesus.

Prayer:
Dear Lord, please give me wisdom and opportunities to teach my children, grandchildren, and other young people about You. Amen.

My restorer

*Y*our righteousness reaches to the skies, O God, you who have done great things. Who, O God, is like you? Though you have made me see troubles, many and bitter, you will restore my life again; from the depths of the earth you will again bring me up. You will increase my honour and comfort me once again. *Psalm 71:19–21*

Reminding ourselves of God's character and of His mighty deeds in the past is a good way of lifting our spirits if we should feel down at any time. There is no one like God! In this passage the psalmist looks back to the past, remembering troubles he has been through. But then he puts those aside and looks forward confidently to the future. He firmly believes that his life will be restored. The 'depths of the earth' is a reference to death or the grave. This elderly man is facing the fact that one day he will die and be buried. That is not the end, however; God will raise him up to a new life where there will be no enemies to torment him and he will be comforted in God's presence.

Prayer:
Dear Lord God, thank You that I can trust You with my life. Thank You that You have always been with me, and will one day raise me up to a new life. Amen.

My God, Holy One

I will praise you with the harp for your faithfulness, O my God; I will sing praise to you with the lyre, O Holy One of Israel. My lips will shout for joy when I sing praise to you – I, whom you have redeemed. My tongue will tell of your righteous acts all day long, for those who wanted to harm me have been put to shame and confusion. *Psalm 71:22–24*

The psalm ends with an outburst of praise. Notice the different ways the psalmist expresses his praise to God – he uses musical instruments, he shouts for joy, he sings and he tells others about God's acts. Think about how you can praise God – when you are on your own, when you are with other people or in church. It is tempting to grumble, to talk about our aches and pains and the difficult time we are having, and sometimes it is right to share our problems with friends. Always, though, it is good to praise God.

Praise Him for His faithfulness, His loving care, His righteousness. Praise Him for Jesus, for His sacrifice, His risen life, redeeming power, forgiveness and certain hope for the future. Praise Him for the beauties of creation.

Praise Him all day long.

Prayer:
Holy God, I praise You for Your glory, Your majesty, and Your wonderful love. Amen.

To know Christ

*Y*et whatever gains I had, these I have come to regard as loss because of Christ. More than that, I regard everything as loss because of the surpassing value of knowing Christ Jesus my Lord. For his sake I have suffered the loss of all things, and I regard them as rubbish, in order that I may gain Christ and be found in him, not having a righteousness of my own that comes from the law, but one that comes through faith in Christ, the righteousness from God based on faith. I want to know Christ ...
Philippians 3:7–10a (NRSV)

The apostle Paul was in prison when he wrote this letter to the church at Philippi. He had lost all things materially because of his faith in Christ. Before his conversion he had held a high position in the Jewish community, but now Paul's one aim in life was to know and serve his Lord, Jesus Christ.

Knowing a person is not just being aware of all the facts about them. It is like knowing a partner or a best friend – knowing what they are thinking and how to please them. We can know Jesus like that by taking time every day to pray, to read His Word and to do His will.

Prayer:
Dear Lord Jesus, please help me to know You better day by day. Amen.

Press on

I press on to make [the goal] my own, because Christ Jesus has made me his own. Beloved, I do not consider that I have made it my own; but this one thing I do: forgetting what lies behind and straining forward to what lies ahead, I press on towards the goal for the prize of the heavenly call of God in Christ Jesus.
Philippians 3:12b–14 (NRSV)

All of us who are mature should take such a view of things. Even after many years of missionary work, Paul was still pressing on to know Christ better. He often uses examples from the world of athletics, and as we think of the modern Olympic Games, we can see the dedicated single-mindedness of the athletes as they prepare and compete to win medals. Athletes do not think of past failures but constantly strive to reach the goal – to be the best they can be. Paul was pressing on to know Christ, to be like Him, and ultimately to win the prize for which God had called Him – everlasting glory in heaven with Christ.

There is no better aim in life than that.

Prayer:
Lord Jesus Christ, I want to follow Paul's example, to forget past failures and to press on to know You better. Thank You that one day I will see You face to face in heaven, and be with You always. Amen.